America's Greatness
From A to Shining Z

ASL Coloring Book

by Maddy Dean

1 Smart Cookie Publications

U.S.A.

Dedicated to

Bruce, Keith, Isaac, and all the other men and women of the U.S. military, past and present. Thank you for serving to protect and defend the United States from all enemies foreign and domestic. America is still a free nation because of your dedication and bravery.

Copyright

Copyright © 2024 by Maddy Dean
All rights reserved

Bibliographical Note

America's Greatness, from A to Shining Z: ASL Coloring Book is a new work, first published by 1 Smart Cookie Publications in 2024

International Standard Book Number
ISBN-13: 979-8-9900396-0-5

AMERICAN GREATNESS

CAN BE DESCRIBED IN ONE WORD:

FREEDOM!

But are younger generations still taught about American exceptionalism??

A QUESTION BEST ANSWERED BY PRESIDENT REAGAN IN HIS 1989 FAREWELL ADDRESS TO THE NATION:

"An informed patriotism is what we want. And are we doing a good enough job teaching our children what America is and what she represents in the long history of the world? Those of us who are over 35 or so years of age grew up in a different America. We were taught, very directly, what it means to be an American. And we absorbed, almost in the air, a love of country and an appreciation of its institutions...

But now, we're about to enter the nineties, and some things have changed. Younger parents aren't sure that an unambivalent appreciation of America is the right thing to teach modern children. And as for those who create the popular culture, well-grounded patriotism is no longer the style. Our spirit is back, but we haven't reinstitutionalized it.

We've got to do a better job of getting across that America is freedom -- freedom of speech, freedom of religion, freedom of enterprise. And freedom is special and rare. It's fragile; it needs [protection]."

This coloring book is designed to shine a light on the greatness of America and enlighten today's youth about how extraordinary this country was in the past and can continue to be in the future. At the same time, this book also teaches the fundamentals of American Sign Language, which will be an essential skill to communicate with the growing number of those with autism and other disabilities.

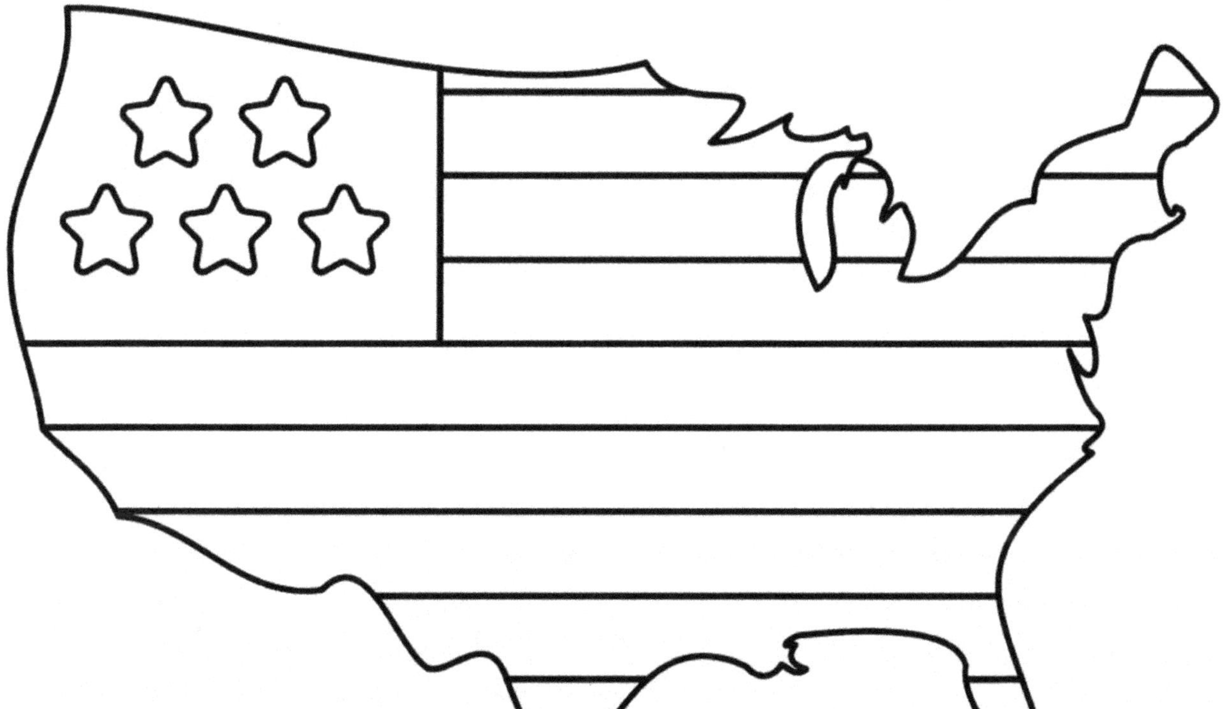

When America was first founded, it consisted of 13 colonies. As the settlers moved away from the east coast, 37 more states were established. Can you name all 50 states?

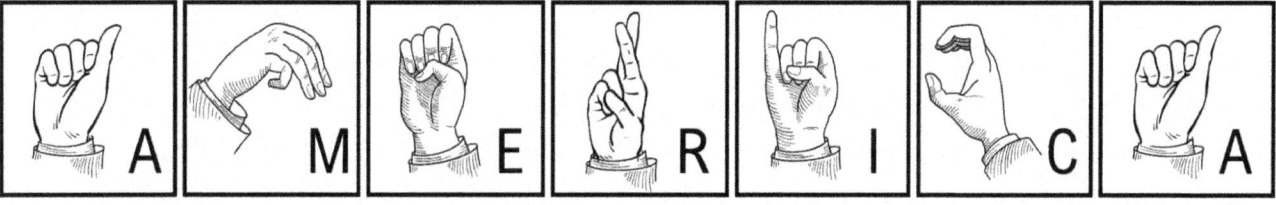

While sailing around the world in 1492, Italian explorer Christopher Columbus discovered America.

CHRISTOPHER

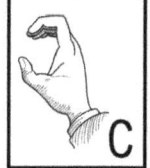 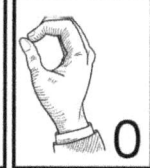   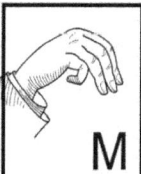 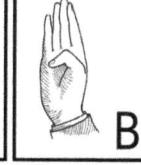  

C O L U M B U S

The Ford Motor Company was founded in Detroit, Michigan. In 1908, Henry Ford proudly introduced his Model T automobile to an eagerly awaiting nation. On the heels of Ford's success, General Motors and Chrysler also opened manufacturing plants in Detroit, earning it the new nickname, "Motor City". In 1960, Berry Gordy, Jr. started Motown Records in this same booming community. Mr. Gordy was one of the most successful black businessmen of all time. He signed on to his music label, legends like Stevie Wonder, Jackson 5, Temptations, Four Seasons, and Diana Ross & the Supremes.

Located in New York Harbor, this island is now home to the National Museum of Immigration and is open to the public.

E L L I S

I S L A N D

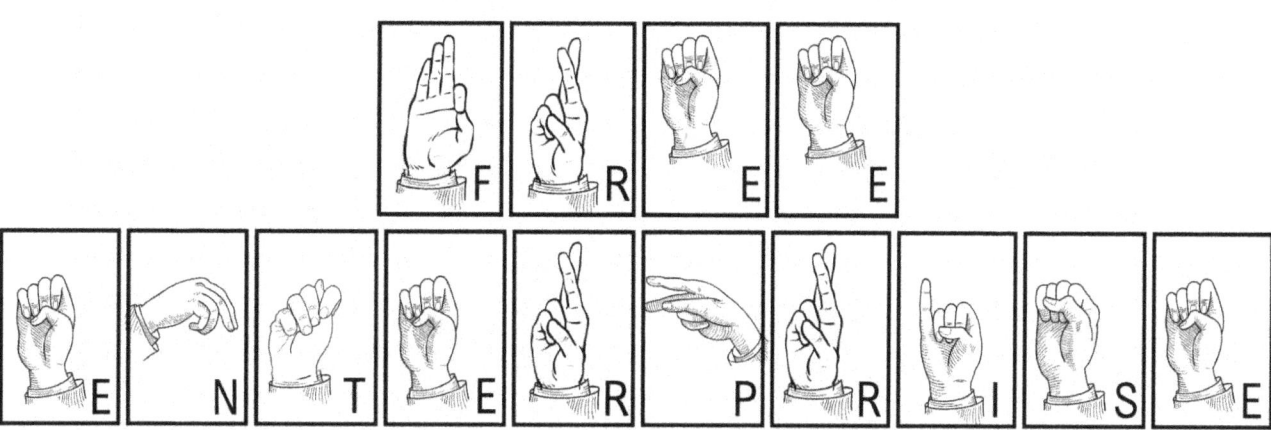

In America, you can start your own business without the government standing in your way. This is called Free Enterprise.
What kind of business would you like to own?

F R E E

E N T E R P R I S E

George Washington was the first President of the United States of America, one of the Founding Fathers, and Commander of the Continental Army.

G E O R G E

W A S H I N G T O N

Washington D. C. is the home of America's Capitol. It is here where elected officials of Congress gather to write new laws, vote, hold hearings, and are supposed to regulate government spending. The Senate and the House of Representatives are the two bodies of Congress, each meeting on separate sides of this building. Capitol Hill is also known as "The People's House" because the elected representatives work for "We the People".

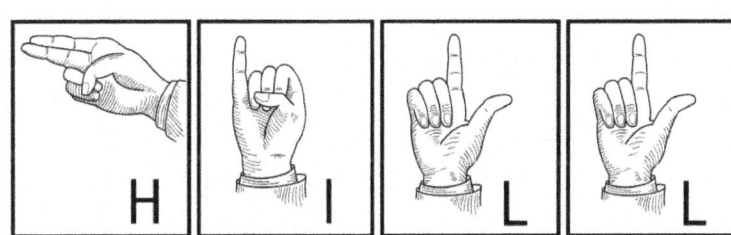

CAPITOL   H   I   L   L

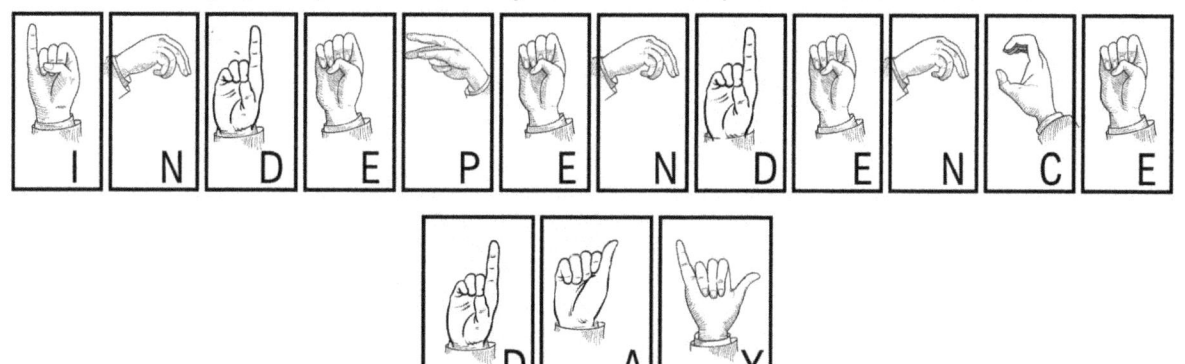

On July 4, 1776, America officially declared its independence from Great Britain.

INDEPENDENCE

DAY

John Hancock was the first person to sign the Declaration of Independence. It is rumored that he signed his name in large letters because he wanted to be certain his signature could be seen by the English King (without the King's reading glasses).

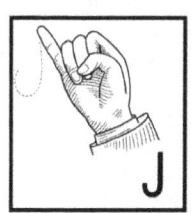 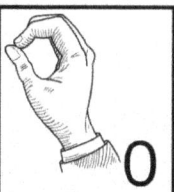 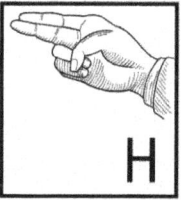 

J O H N

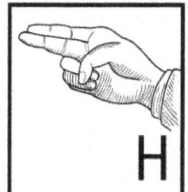 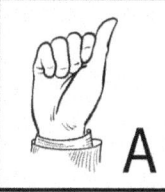  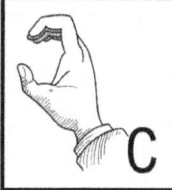  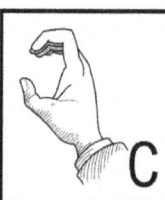 

H A N C O C K

In Louisville, Kentucky, at the Churchill Downs stadium, America's oldest sporting event occurs each year on the first Saturday of May. The Kentucky Derby is also known as the "Run for the Roses".

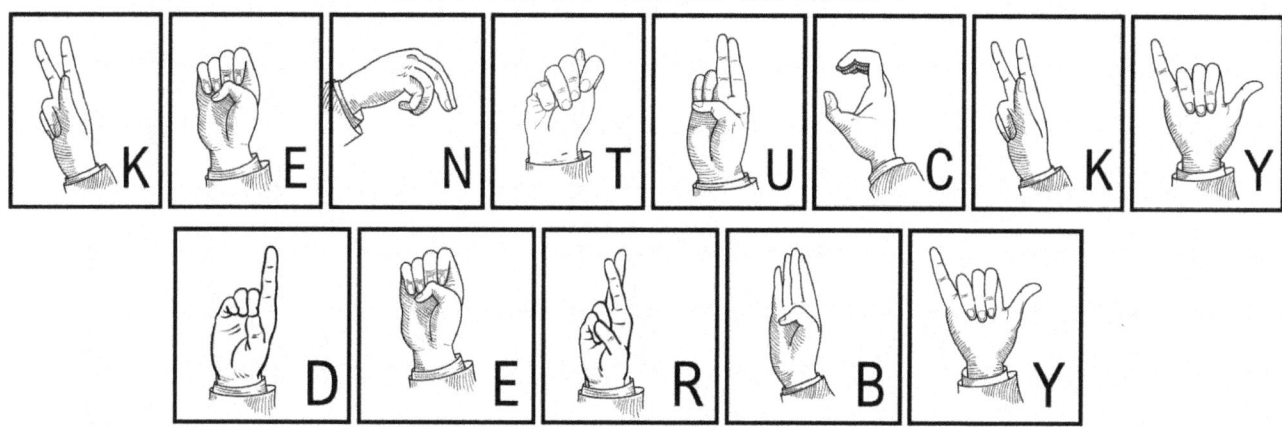

K E N T U C K Y

D E R B Y

LIBERTY BELL

This historic symbol of freedom and justice can be viewed in Philadelphia, Pennsylvania. Written on the top of the bell is the eternal message, "Proclaim Liberty Throughout All the Land Unto All the Inhabitants thereof". This verse is from the King James version of the Bible (Leviticus 25:10).

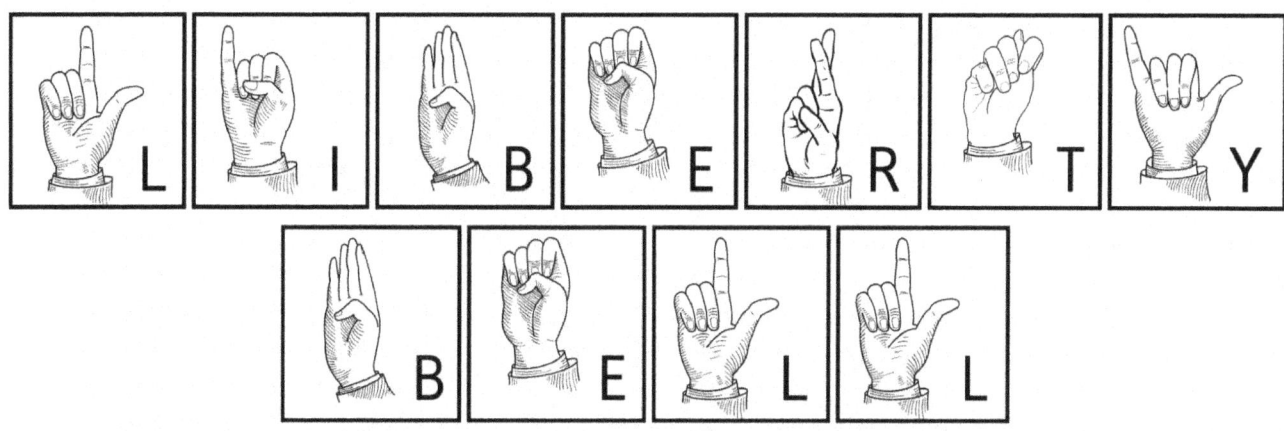

Located in South Dakota, this national monument features the faces of four famous Presidents: George Washington, Thomas Jefferson, Theodore Roosevelt, and Abraham Lincoln.

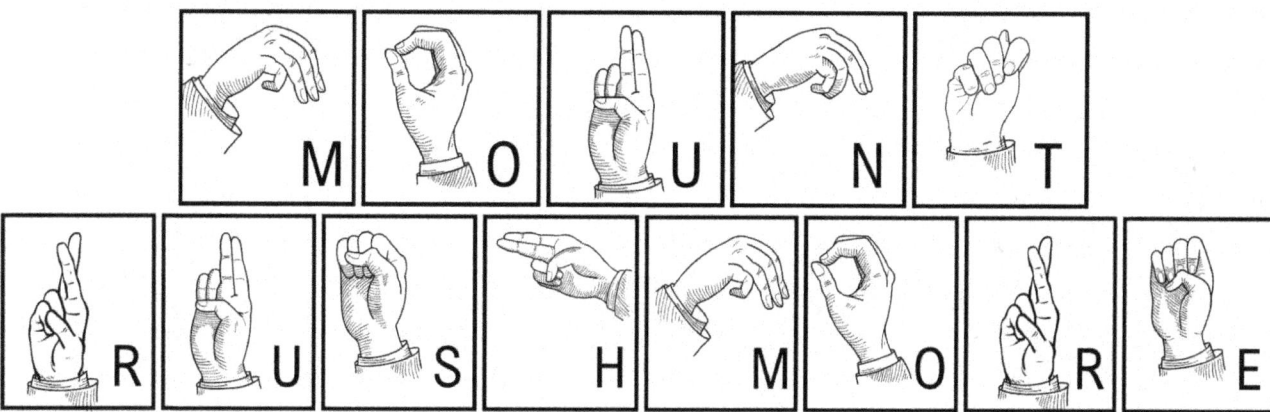

M O U N T

R U S H M O R E

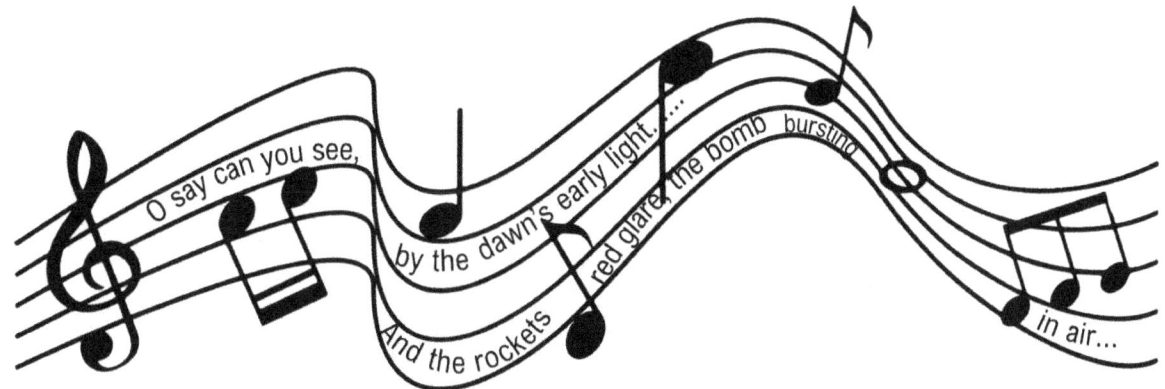

THE STAR-SPANGLED BANNER

During the War of 1812 with Great Britain, Francis Scott Key wrote the Star-Spangled Banner. Congress adopted it as America's National Anthem in 1931.

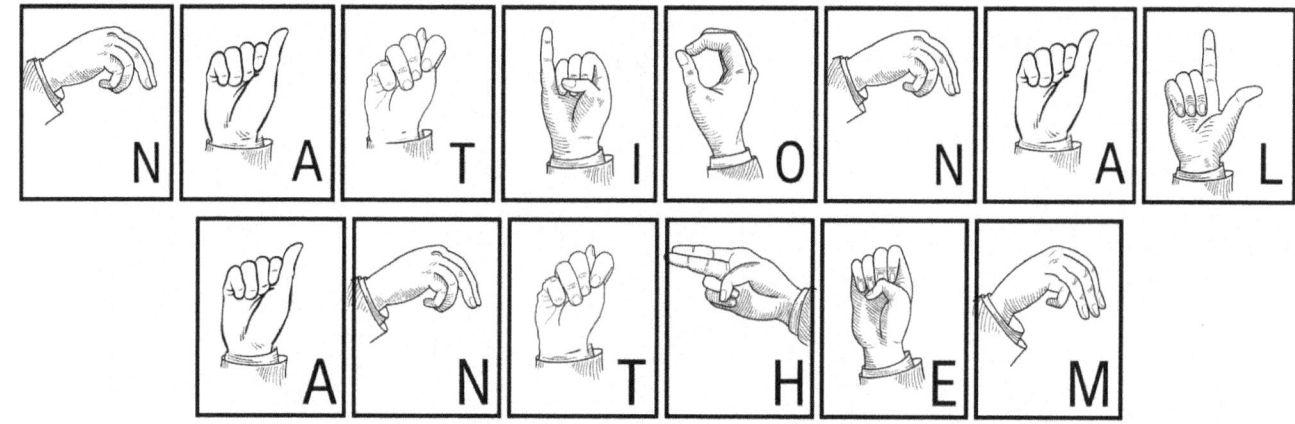

The American Flag is also known as "Old Glory". It has 50 stars, one per state, and each of its 13 stripes represents one of the original colonies.

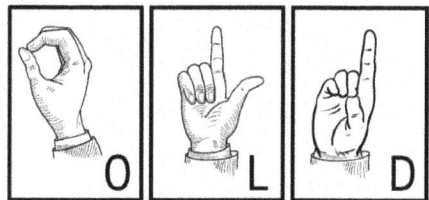

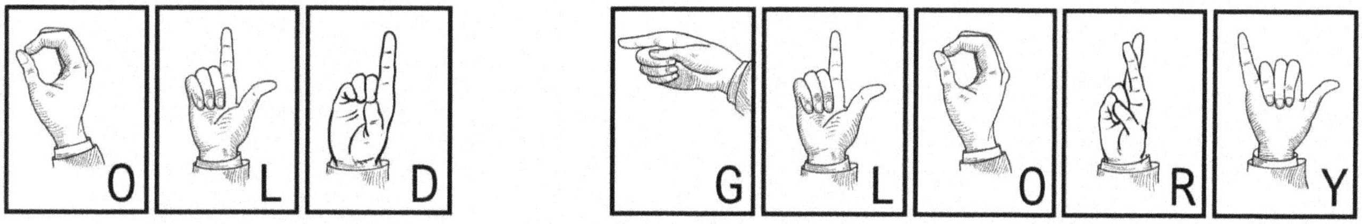

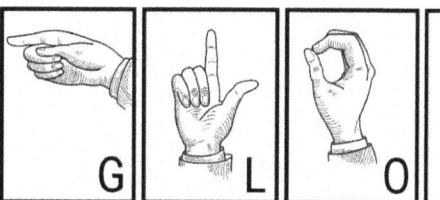

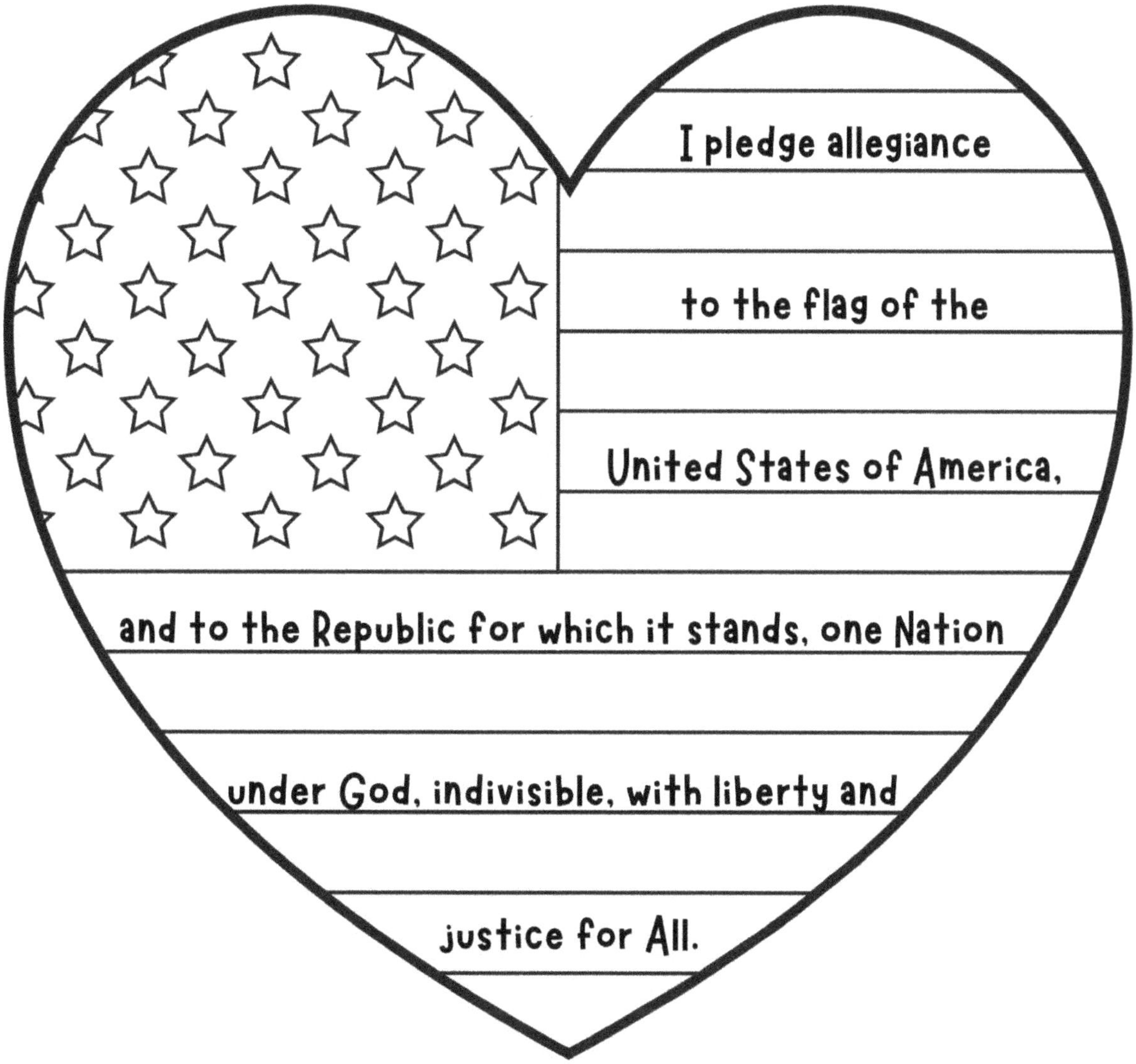

I pledge allegiance
to the flag of the
United States of America,
and to the Republic for which it stands, one Nation
under God, indivisible, with liberty and
justice for All.

The proper way to say the Pledge is to stand at attention, face the American flag, and place your right hand over your heart. Some places the Pledge is recited include grade school classrooms, government meetings and hearings, veteran-related events, and citizenship ceremonies.

P L E D G E
O F
A L L E G I A N C E

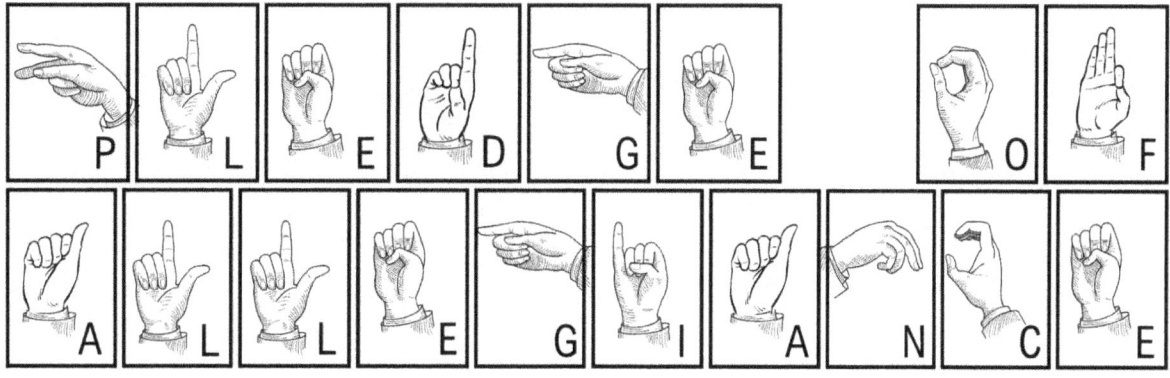

The U.S. currently has six unique coins in circulation - penny, nickel, dime, quarter, half-dollar, and $1 coin (for collector purposes only).

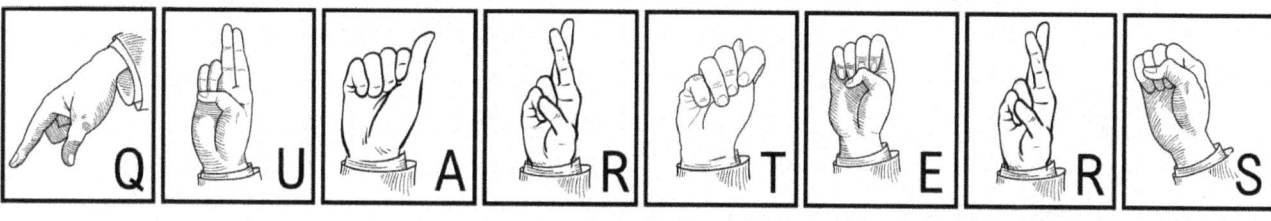

Q U A R T E R S

NATIONAL FLOWER

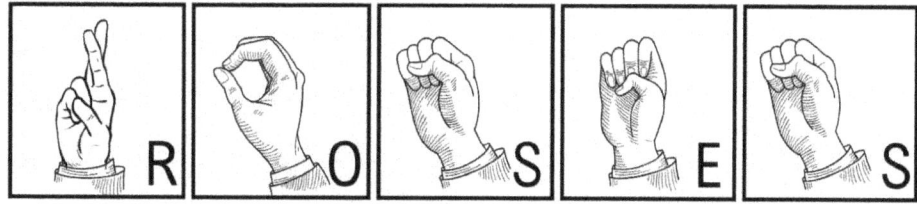

Standing tall while she holds her torch up high, Lady Liberty is the true beacon of freedom to all who see her. She was a gift from France and was shipped to America in 214 crates. The year was 1885. A dedication of the completed Statue took place in October 1886 by President Grover Cleveland. In New York, you can visit this magnificent landmark on Liberty Island.

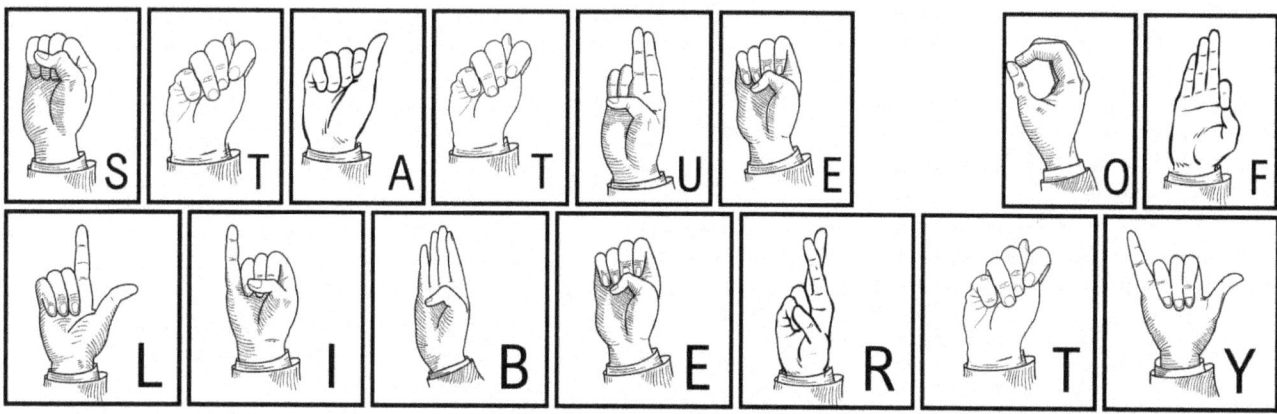

After the pilgrims came to America on the Mayflower, they shared their first harvest with the Native Americans in 1621. Reportedly, this first Thanksgiving lasted three days. In 1863, President Abraham Lincoln declared Thanksgiving a National holiday. In part, he said in his Proclamation, "... to set apart and observe the last Thursday of November next, as a day of Thanksgiving and Praise to our beneficent Father who dwelleth in the Heavens".

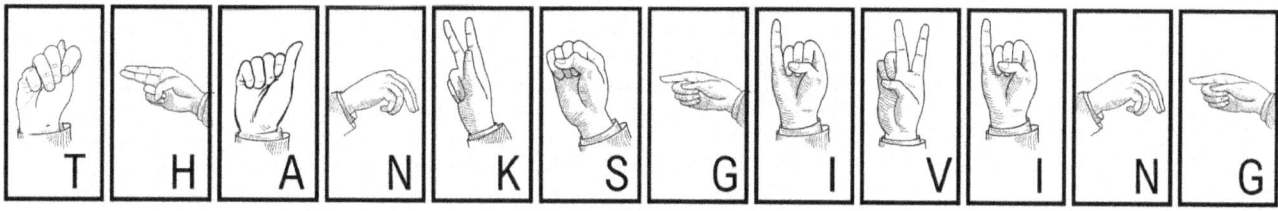

T H A N K S G I V I N G

The Constitution of the United States

We the people of the United States, in order to form a more perfect Union, establish Justice, insure domestic Tranquility, provide for the common defense, promote the general Welfare, and secure the Blessings of Liberty to ourselves and our Posterity, do ordain and establish this Constitution for the United States of America.

The United States Constitution was signed on September 17, 1787, establishing the government structure of America. Even though there have been 27 Amendments to this document, the Constitution remains the highest law in the land. All of your rights as an American citizen are spelled out within the pages of the U.S. Constitution. How many of those rights can you name?

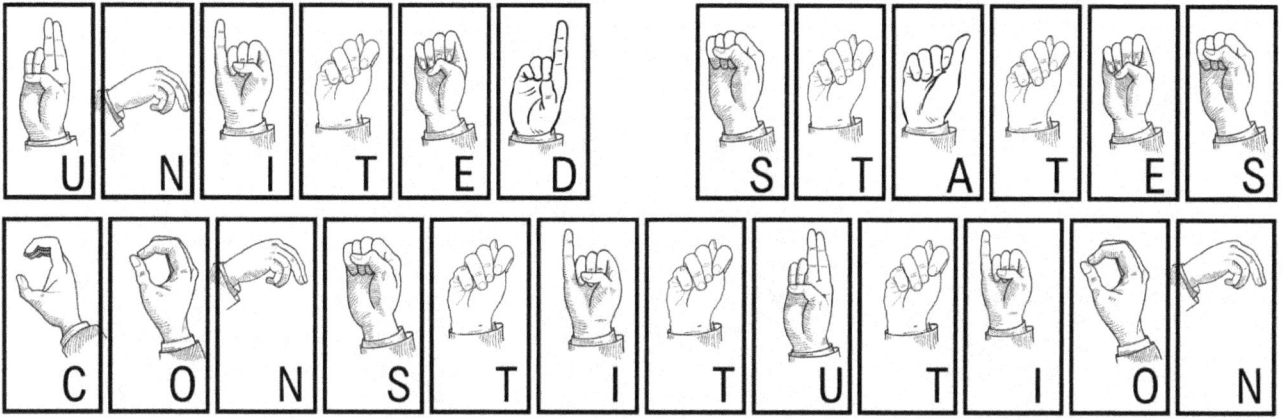

U N I T E D S T A T E S

C O N S T I T U T I O N

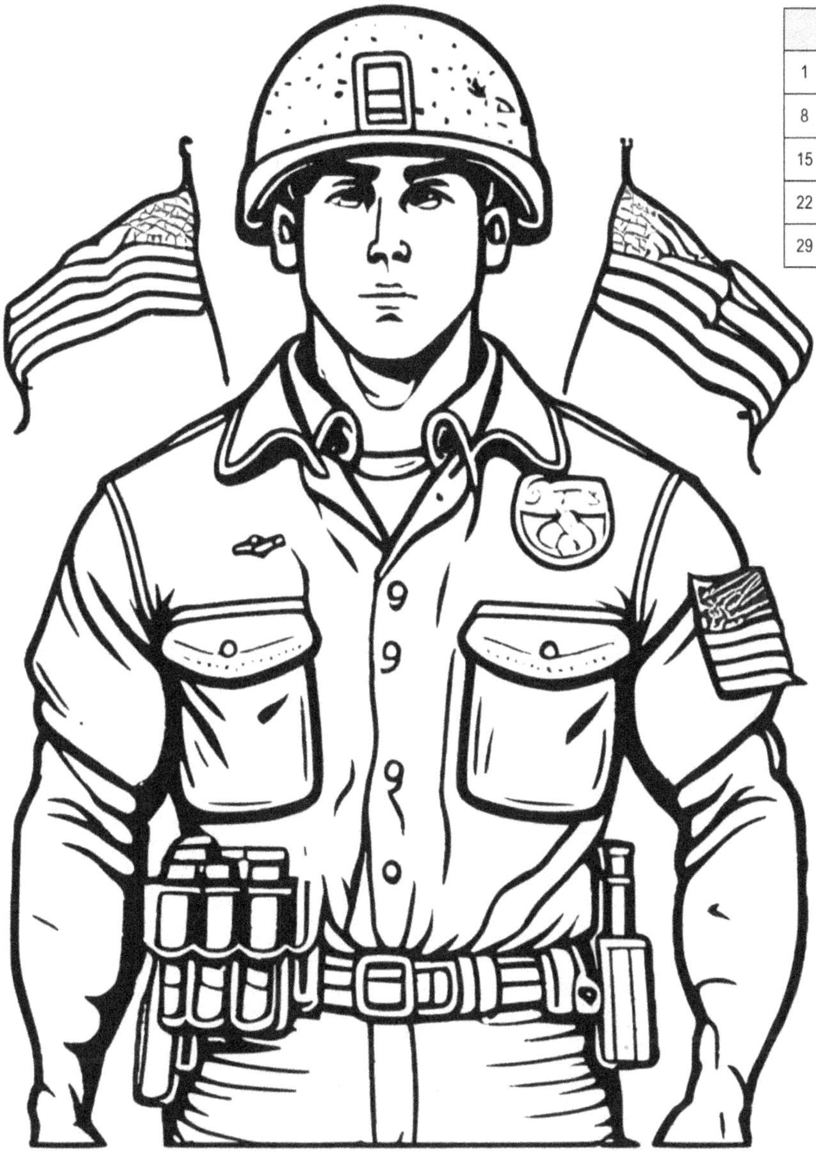

Every year on November 11, America pays tribute to the men and women who served in the United States military. Veterans Day is for all six branches of the U.S. military - Army, Navy, Marine Corps, Air Force, Coast Guard, and Space Force. Do you have any relatives who have served in the military?

V E T E R A N S

D A Y

While in Washington D.C., you can visit the current President's home, also known as the "White House".

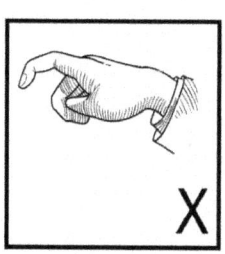 Formerly known as "Twitter", the world's largest social media company has been renamed "X" by its American owner, Elon Musk. Currently, "X" is headquartered in California.

In California, Yosemite National Park encompasses almost 1,200 square miles of mountainous terrain, high waterfalls, deep valleys, and thick wilderness.

    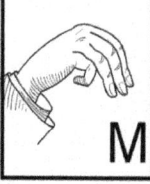 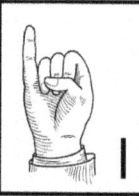  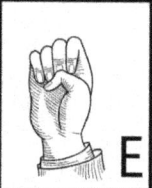

Y O S E M I T E

ASL Review Sheet

A	B	C	D
E	F	G	H
I	J	K	L
M	N	O	P
Q	R	S	T
U	V	W	X
Y	Z		

Is America a Republic or Democracy?

"What's the difference?"

A **Democracy** is a government based on a <u>direct</u> vote by the people to change existing laws and policies based on their personal preferences. The majority wins, with no regard for the rule of law - just the people's whims matter.

In a **Republic**, representatives are elected by the people to form a government body. The elected officials <u>represent</u> the citizens by passing laws to govern the country.

ANSWER:

America is a Republic.
The U.S. Constitution confirms this in Article 4, Section 4, stating, "The United States shall guarantee to every State in this Union a Republican Form of Government...". Ben Franklin famously declared America is a Republic and not a Democracy. In addition, the Pledge of Allegiance states, "...and to the *Republic* for which it stands, one Nation, under God..."

As the framers wrote the Constitution and formed the U.S. Government, they turned to the Bible for guidance - especially referring to the following verse found in Exodus 18:21

Furthermore, you shall select out of all the people able men who fear God, men of truth, those who hate dishonest gain; and you shall place these over them as leaders of thousands, of hundreds, of fifties and of tens. (NASB1995)

US Constitutional Amendments

"Do you know your Constitutional rights? Let's review some of them."

1st Amendment
Freedom of speech, religion and press. You have the right to peaceably assemble.

2nd Amendment
It gives you the right to own weapons, including guns, to protect yourself from a tyrannical government.

4th Amendment
Protects you and your property from all unreasonable searches & seizures.

6th Amendment
If charged with a crime, the accused shall enjoy the right to a speedy and public trial, and witnesses are allowed to testify on the behalf of the accused.

19th Amendment
As of 1920, all women were given the right to vote.

9th Amendment
Covers all other rights not directly addressed in the Constitution, like a person's right to privacy.

14th Amendment
All persons born in the United States automatically become U.S. citizens at birth.

26th Amendment
All citizens of the United States, who are 18 years of age or older, have the right to vote and that right shall not be denied or abridged by the United States or by any State on account of age.

13th Amendment
Slavery or involuntary servitude, except as a punishment for crime whereof the party shall have been duly convicted, shall not exist within the United States.

US STATES MAP

AL Alabama
AK Alaska
AZ Arizona
AR Arkansas
CA California
CO Colorado
CT Connecticut *
DE Delaware *
FL Florida
GA Georgia *
HI Hawaii
ID Idaho
IL Illinois
IN Indiana
IA Iowa
KS Kansas
KY Kentucky
LA Louisiana
ME Maine
MD Maryland *
MA Massachusetts *
MI Michigan
MN Minnesota
MS Mississippi
MO Missouri
MT Montana
NE Nebraska
NV Nevada
NH New Hampshire *
NJ New Jersey *
NM New Mexico
NY New York *
NC North Carolina *
ND North Dakota
OH Ohio
OK Oklahoma
OR Oregon
PA Pennsylvania *
RI Rhode Island *
SC South Carolina *
SD South Dakota
TN Tennessee
TX Texas
UT Utah
VT Vermont
VA Virginia *
WA Washington
WV West Virginia
WI Wisconsin
WY Wyoming

(*) Indicates the original 13 colonies

<u>Find your state on the above map and color it in.</u>

In which year was your state established? _____

In which city is your state capitol? _____

What is the name of your state bird? _____

What is the name of your state flower? _____

What are the colors of your state flag? _____

www.ingramcontent.com/pod-product-compliance
Lightning Source LLC
Chambersburg PA
CBHW081455060426
42444CB00037BA/3295